Allergies: Poems on Grieving and Loving

Allergies: Poems on Grieving and Loving

Maggie Bowyer

Maggie Bowyer
Greensboro, North Carolina
www.maggiebowyer.com
hello@maggiewrites.com

ISBN: 9798987027707
Printed in the United States of America
First Printing, 2022

To the kinds of love that make grieving possible

Winter

Allergens

I was born allergic to milk;
My first day on Earth
I was already spitting up
Nutrients in favor of processed.
It is no wonder my brain
Was grated down into slivers
Not big enough to choke on
But not tasty enough to devour.
A large part of me wonders if I was
Always destined to repel
The very things that are best for me -
Do I lack the vitamins and grit
It takes to make it in this world?
Was I doomed from birth or
Is that a self-fulfilling prophecy,
A way to turn away from nourishment?
I guess in the end,
It all tastes like resentment.

My bones crunch under
The pressure of a slow
Transformation into stone.
They rattle inside me;
Making music
Out of my misery
Is the only solace
This body can give me.

Finding Out

I don't remember the last time
We locked eyes, your blue
Coming   to meet my green -
I don't know if it was when you
Were last framed by my thighs,
Maybe when I saw you across the colosseum
The day your brother graduated,
Or the first ~~- and last -~~ time I lied to you,
Screaming I hate you, or at least
The lack of having you.
I refuse to count when I stared
At the picture of you in the paper,
Bore a hole in the table
After the first hour,
Still not fully understanding
The same six sentences.
Are you looking after me?

Roller Coaster

You said
"I'm sorry honey,
But it's time to go."

No matter how many
Downs were between
Each of our ups,
I'm left desperate
For one more ride.

Funeral Juxtaposition

We stand far too close,
Baby hairs on forearms brushing,
Breath mint clouds
Prickling on our necks.
Everyone leans in,
Feasting on the words
Of a preacher who'd
Never even met her.
The pews weren't as stiff
As my words were
Reciting the Lord's Prayer
In my mother's name.
There was no burial,
As the only wish honored
Was her incineration.
After hugs full of
Too much perfume,
Stiff, freshly pressed suits,
And tears from relatives who
Meant relatively nothing to me,
We went home.
Laid out on the counters
Were ham biscuits
And cold cuts.
The room was filled

With the smell of meat
I refused to eat,
And the chatter of wrinkled lips
"Catching up"
Between bites of
Too sweet brownies.
No one noticed
Me slip off my heels
And out the door.
I couldn't be there,
Where no one seemed to recall
How we just stared at
A seemingly plastic corpse,
My mom's hair completely wrong,
In her least favorite outfit.
So I sat outside,
In the grass,
Feeling the sting
Of a late December rain.
I ruined that dress,
The black one with
Small purple flowers,
The one I was supposed to
Wear to her wedding.
The rain seemed fitting;
She only liked to leave the beach
On rainy days.

My grandparents sat inside,
Forgetting storms of their own,
While I shared malice
With the clouds above.
I don't know how
You end a poem
About your mother's death
This quick,
Much like I don't know how God
Ends a mother's life
When she was only 36.

I just want -
No,
I just need
A moment
To rest.
To catch
My breath,
Gone missing,
As impossible
To find as wind.
I'm just going
To lie down
For a while,
Maybe longer.

Red light.

Yellow light.

That very first night,
You grabbed my hand and
Spun me to a traffic light party.

That green dress looks
Beautiful on you,
Your lashes fluttered -
I was immediately flustered.

Your arm around my waist,
Wrapped in greenery,
I should have seen the
Red flags flying
And red lights flashing -
You were going to pass me
Around like a water bottle
Full of vodka you never
Had any intention of finishing,
Just wanted the green light
And a few years of my life.

Almost Was Never Enough, Huh?

There was this great pause
After "You know, these days
I have been drifting away."
I almost snatch the silence
From the space between us.
I almost beg you to stay.
I almost remind you of my ghost,
The one who danced on a rooftop
With their top off,
Top of the world;
I almost remind you
Of how late you stayed,
With your jacket warming me
And your arms supporting me.

I almost lay the words
"I never stopped loving you,"
On the table - but then I realize
I am still lying.

Bad Night (1)

I broke down
The day I realized
I have to exist
On the same planet
As you -
Forever.

Inventory

A friend once told me
That everything is made up
Of masses of atoms
Wavering at incalculable speeds;
Our electrons only ever
Hit constant resistance.
"We never truly touch anything,"
He said.
I attempted to lock my quivering fingers
Around my mother's wedding dress -
I'm not sure
If it was the electrons in my palms
Or the fact that my hands
Aren't big enough to catch all of this grief,
But my fingers refused to latch on.
She is gone,
And my muscles aren't strong enough
To rip open everything that now haunts me,
Cardboard blockades against every memory
Sprouting up around me.
Each item I dredge from these boxes
Tugs on my biceps,
Adding to the burden on my shoulders:
CDs, dishes, sweaters,
Paintings blenders journals

Photos mixed tapes bed frames
Jewelry lotion silverware,
An entire house is now on my back!
She is gone and all that she left were
CDs she'd owned since she was 16,
Full of songs we'd belted out on road trips;
Every time I drive I hear
You and me baby we're stuck like glue
Wahoo wahoo stuck like glue, you and me
Baby we're stuck like glue;
Parent Trap and Freaky Friday,
All the movies we'd binged on
During all of those sick days;
Packages full of pounds of pills,
Stuffed with questions on if they
Healed her or killed her;
Merrily wrapped Christmas presents
Screaming for celebration,
These ghosts of gifts she never got to give.
She died on Christmas Eve -
These ghosts of gifts
Never seemed so ironic to me.
As slowly as I remove
Each item from these boxes,
I realize
I will never have the present
Of her presence again.

She is gone and she will never
See another Christmas, birthday, performance,
Prom, graduation, my wedding...
She will never me her grandkids....
She is gone and will never
Take another photo of me,
Her shaking hands capturing
Every fuzzy memory;
She is gone but please
Do not say this to me
Because I'm doing my best
To live in my bubble of disillusion,
Untouched by the truth
In your words,
But in reality
Those words -
She is gone -
Shatter me,
And I spend my nights in bed
Imagining her mud buddies
On my tongue,
Begging God
"Send my mommy home,
Send me one last embrace
Of her electrons,"
Because she is gone,
And my atoms cannot bear this

Genetic separation,
But if all of this were based on science
Just like he said,
Then these emotions boil down
To simple chemical imbalances,
Yet I would give everything
To invent a time machine,
Fall through the years,
And dance with her again.

When I sent you away,
I never meant it to be for good.

I Thought We Were In Love

I pulled him into me
No matter how little
I wanted to be in my skin,
Much less have someone
Else's skin against mine.
I tried my best to satisfy,
To work up ~~desire~~ courage
To feel daggers slide into me
And pretend I was interested.
I bit my tongue until it bled
Just like my lips,
Clenched my legs tight
Once he had left me vacant
And throbbing -
I never let him see
The way he made me bleed,
The pain inflicted every time
We were intimate.
I wonder if that's why
I grew to resent him,
In the end.

I think I lost the last three years
Somewhere along my way home;
When I went looking,
I realized I misplaced
The last four,
Five,
Six...
Frankly, I'm not sure
How to tell
If I ever existed.

Good Mourning

It was not cold muffins,
Crumbs left on my breakfast bar.
It was not cold bedsheets
After he left me sleeping.

It was nothing.
We were nothing.

It was not cold muffins
Because he didn't stay for breakfast
And neither did my appetite.
It was not cold sheets
Because we spent
Less than ten minutes
Buried in them.

It is cold hands
Clutched around phone screens,
Because the ability
To reveal everything
Has become easier digitally.
I thought it was just sex to me.
This was supposed to be
Parents aren't home
And fun with camera phones.

I was under the impression
That he agreed with me,
But I am colder than I once was.

Quickly, the occasional quickie
Turned into two-hour layovers
Where I laid over his chest,
Invested in the ways
He had broken bones
And cracked his heart.
We sat for hours
Passing each other
The smallest bits of ourselves;
In between elbow banging
He told me
He was scared of liver failure
And all the ways
He failed his mother;
I gave him all the parts of me
My father had abandoned,
Tied together with all my insecurities,
The shape of my pinkie toes,
And the way I talk too loudly.

We gave each other everything.
We were still nothing.

He doesn't like baked goods.
Bed sheets are no longer cold.
I thought that he knew
This was just sex,
But now I'm getting seven texts
And three phone calls
Waking me up,
My groggy voice answering
"Hello?"
He was upset,
My ears still stuffed with
Cotton balls and dreams
Heard only silence.
It is 12:06
On June third,
The clock won't stop
Reminding him she overdosed
Three years ago today.
He blames himself.
She was his first love,
First to make love,
To break love.

I am realizing
Sleeping in beds
Makes them warmer.
We began sleeping closer.

He warned me that
He was the plot twist
In her downward spiral.
I tried to tell him
People hit rock bottom
Even when they're not pushed.

It was never just sex,
As we laid in bed
Our shaking hands reaching
For frigid sheets
To cover vacant bodies.
He'd forgotten how to love
And I had forgotten
It was never me
He was reaching for;
I forgot to care.
I wish it was still just sex,
The same way I wish
I had burnt those muffins
And wish we never
Even made it to the bed;
Maybe then we wouldn't remember
How cold these sheets used to be.

It was nothing.
I wish we weren't still nothing.

It is the morning after,
Snuggling into icy beds
With no one next to me
And waking up too tired
To bake muffins.

He is still mourning.
I am waiting.

How many ghosts attended
Your graduation ceremony?
Could you hear their
      (broken) harmony?

Blue Book

Did you only show up for me?
To bring me a $3.29 veggie burger?
Sat down at the exam as though
All was going as planned -
An assured confidence
You assured me would get you killed.
Filled the whole page with lead,
Spent the entire essay hour
Adding incalculable coats.

Why take the test if you aren't
At least attempting an essay?

Did you only show up for me?
To bring me fast food?
I wish I would have asked you
To color me in like I am a blue book,
Study me like a test,
Memorize me like you're the one
About to memorialize me,
Turn down your charisma
Before it got you killed.

I am grappling with the part of myself
That believes I'm not worth
Even the tiniest bit of love.

He is a sleep fighter;
His idea of rest resembles
Wrestling while unconscious.
He throws punches
As though they are pillows;
He's a blanket hog too.
Make no mistake,
While his slumber can lead
To unintended injuries,
There is not a violent bone
In that boy's body.
If you are sharing his bed,
Know there is not a malicious
Thought in his head;
You'll know you're family
When his goodbyes
Are simply *love*;
You are one of the luckiest
Girls in the world.
Lay some pillows on the floor
For when he pushes you
Off the edge, and know he will
Pick you up in the morning.
Let him get a full 10 hours,
And make sure you shower
Him with enough compassion
He can leave the fighting
In his dreams.

I write these poems so I won't
Forget your nuances -
How am I supposed to
Hold onto you
For a whole lifetime?

Where Can You Hide From Your Fears?

Parts of you still linger,
Finding flecks of your blue
In the eyes of every passing stranger;
I'm still overwhelmed by your presence
Months after your absence,
Like my aunt's perfume when she hugged me
Close enough to leave lipstick in my hair.
I wish I could forget your existence,
But my mind won't stop insisting
I drive straight across town,
Down your cul-de-sac and up your driveway,
Knock on your side door,
Blow past your mom,
Words already spilling from my lips,
"I know you don't know me,
But your son meant everything
To someone who felt like nothing -
He brought me a veggie burger
In between my two exams
Even though I asked by calling him a ham.
He never held it against me
When I didn't want to be held.
When the lights in your driveway broke?
He told you he hit them with the lawnmower,
When really it was me, in a rush, a flush

After he kissed me. I couldn't stop
Looking at him in the porch light,
But he didn't want me to feel guilty.
I want you to know that he wasn't
Just some junkie, he really
Meant something to someone,
Even if it ended up being nothing."
Instead of spewing a monologue,
I put on some talk show
To drown out the blame bouncing between
The rock and the hard place in my brain.
The fears you hid inside of me
Finally became a reality.

Goddammit, I Miss You So Much
After Laura Jean Henebry

Who else drops everything the Sunday after Christmas to show
up to a hollow house and roll a blunt? Let nuggets fall on the
carpet; *you can light up in here because she used to anyway, who
will know the difference?*

Who else spends every waking minute trying to garner laughter
from those around him? He was all funny bones, bickered with
the ladies around him, colored in essays with crayons, winked
across the pool at me (I hoped no one saw but these days I regret
sneaking around; secrets feel a lot like lying now)

Who else knows to push me up against the wall when they kiss
me? Wrapped his hand in my hair, snaked the other around my
waist; even when he was wasted he spent a few gentle hours
worshiping my hips, only taking breaks for water or Marlboro
Red 100's

Who else wants to nothing more than to die but desperately reeks
of life? I honestly never thought he would kick it despite the
white lighter and pushing the speed limit

Who else would I miss like this?

The One

Did they really get away
If they met you at the grave?

We rushed from dark rooms
To pitch-black parking lots;
I saw the dash covered in dust
But kept my nose to myself,
Instead licking papers,
Trying to keep the tray stable
While you drove with your hand
Draped across my ankle.
The irony is, in those days
I already saw you as an angel,
With the halo of the street lamp
Peeking through the smoke
As I beamed at you, arms crossed
Across the basketball court.
Each intersection we blew through
Made me more intent
On riding next to you.
How many nights did you spent
Driving aimlessly,
    Somewhere
    and nowhere
      to be,
    without me?
I hope you found a parking spot
And a little bit of peace.

I tell everyone I have hit
A bit of writer's block,
But it's really memories
I am failing to stop
From pummeling me;
I can't lift the pen
When I am pinned
Under an avalanche
Of unruly emotion,
Coated in a thick
Layer of stringy snot.

Will my words rot
Right here with me?

All I want are butterflies
And baby kicks;
The only thing these contractions
Leave me with is a reminder
These diseases are shredding
And sterilizing me.

Guardian

White feather, tucked
Behind her ear;
White feather, flutter
By me on the street.
White feather, do you ever
Wonder about the weather
Or whether it's raining
Somewhere above the clouds?
White feather, do you ever
Whisper well-wishes
From my mother
When I'm under the weather?
White feather, do you ever
Whistle to my sister
Just to make her giggle
While she waits?
White feather, do you ever
Wander the wisteria
With my little brothers?
White feather, wafting
By my window;
White feather, will you
Remain even when I am a willow?

Do I carry the torch
Of your memory?
I had to bear witness
As you withered;
You vanished before my eyes
And I'm left wondering
If I am the only one who still
Remembers your life.

What Obituaries Forget

We string memories up
To hide the cracks in the walls;
They're paperclipped together,
Fantastically, fundamentally fragile.
We pretend not to notice
All the faces in the photos
We no longer recognize.
Memories cannot be replicated
In the caverns of our mind;
Excavation won't make them tangible.
I'd love to describe her laugh,
But it eludes me;
To tell you all about the way
Her fingers traced the contours of my spine
Would be the greatest joy of mine,
But it just barely escapes me,
Now merely muddled recollections.
Our minds wear
Quicker than photos -
I might know that we sat
Atop a mountain of snow in '02,
But I could never tell you
The shape of the condensation
As it left my mouth,
Or the octave of my father's chuckle

As it reached my ears.
I can recall huddling
In the living room
When the power went out,
Yet I can't accurately describe
Just how her laugh
Warmed the room.
I'm afraid I will never
Accurately honor my mother.

She must've reached out,
Seeking help,
But only found bottles
Offering to solve
Her problems.

There is a strange
Taste on my tongue.
Is it the beginning
Or the ending
That tastes this
Bittersweet?

Cavities

The fridge was buzzing
Something awful in my ear;
The rest of the apartment was eerie,
The silence seeming to bounce
Off the walls now missing
So much of their furniture,
Your furniture.
I turned on a 90s RomCom
To drown out the couple
Arguing about dishes upstairs.
I couldn't help but wonder
Why the fuck all these movies
Always have the heartbroken girl
Shovel Rocky Road into her mouth
While tears dribble down her chin.
The icy brownie bites would remind me
Of the cavity in my back right molar
And your asinine voice would slide
It's way into my ear, "You should
Really schedule that dentist's appointment,"
As if you always showed up
To get your teeth polished every
Six months on the dot.
I'd rather toss a few Rollos into my mouth,
Push them to the back *left* side,

Let them melt just a little bit,
Caramel holding me together.
I turn the volume up to drown out
The voices above getting louder,
Just reminding me I am alone,
Wondering how the girls
In these films always look perfect
When they are crying; I tend to look
Like a clown who got caught
Out in the rainstorm, my balloons
Struck by lightning.
On the screen, the couple,
After each having their own epiphany,
Begin running back to one another -
Running!
I turn off the TV;
I have to get used to the silence.

The good and the present
Will meet again soon.

Wishlist

An automated litter scooper because my back hurts and you already work hard enough / autocorrect for when I misspell litter, and seven other words on the grocery list / a massage gun, or a coupon for your hands on my spine, popping the bubble wrap layer of my muscles / a gift card to the gluten-free bakery downtown and a Saturday morning you'll go with me / these six books, four of which I will inevitably add to your growing "to-read" stack / I would be satisfied if you came home with hot cocoa, the way you did on our first Christmas, and give me a simple kiss / what's on your wishlist?

Yearning for Morning

I ache for the chill exclusive
To five o'clock; my toes
Dance towards the ground,
Awaiting the moment the cool
Concrete meets the balls
Of my blanket-baked feet.
I am eager for my tea, freshest
Before the rest of the world wakes,
Steam rushing to comfort my bones
In the early, ethereal hours;
My body has always reacted poorly
To the billions of people I feel
Bustling around me.

The downtown lights are still on
As I draw my blinds and a bath.
Midnight yet I know millions
Are just beginning their evening,
While I can't wait for morning.

You used to tell me
I didn't know how to spin a story,
Didn't understand the concept
Of a beginning, middle, and

E n d.

Said I couldn't write you a song,
Because you were tired of me
Reading between the lines,
Afraid I'd see through your lies
If we got that intimate.
I've written a few books since then,
All of them about you,
And yet none of them, too.

Funny how we find closure
In chapters but never stories.

Spring

Spring Cleaning

There are five chairs
Covered in pollen
And cluttered in the corner
Of our back porch.
Next weekend we will
Bring out damp cloths
And wipe them off,
Remember that three
Of them have fallen
In on themselves,
Centers missing
Or unstable legs.
You will want to
Load them in my trunk,
Take them to the junkyard;
I will complain about
My allergies bothering me;
We will leave them,
Once again crowding us.
I am always putting off
Letting go of things.

The Bee's Knees

The
    sun
        made
            an
                appearance
yesterday,
    almost exactly a year
since its disappearance.

The flowers
    are mighty

Happy

    and full of fresh rain.

You point out the rainbow
Right above my doorway.

With one touch
I turn to stone;
Wonder how far
I can be thrown.

Grounding

Trapped in a glass cage,
I watch as you create
The perfect day:
Picnic in the park, sunny spot;
Carving pumpkins in the carport;
Walking through the balls of light
The night before Christmas.
The months keep passing
With me, smiling, but still
Far from reality.
I beat on the past, try to shatter
All of my core beliefs, escape
The corner I was boxed into.
I poke at the pieces before me,
Shards of a prism for a prison.
Thank God someone let the light in.

Today I walked outside
To witness an explosion
Of blooms and bees -
Spring has sprung
Where I'm from.

I swear I saw your ghost today

In linen shorts and a shockingly
Mini car ~~no compensation~~
Rolled up casually behind me
At the stop light,
~~stopped me~~
Saw right through me
        through my side mirror.

Why would you haunt the campus
You never made it to?

The air is too sickly sweet for rain,
But then again it is Spring
And the branches are swaying,
Look   now it's pouring
Your scent (how could I forget?)
Mixed with dogwood and water
Comes flooding in my window;
You evaporate in my rearview

Bad Night (2)

I broke down
The day I realized
I have to exist
On a planet
Without you -
Forever.

I want to write
Happy poems.

I want to write
About the mundane shit
That makes life worth
Giving a. single. fuck.

I want to write
About damp clothes
Hung around the apartment
And your arms around my waist.

I want to write
About wasted Saturdays
Because are they really a waste
If they're my favorite days?

I want to stop writing
To let your lips draw near.
I want to tell stories with
My fingers, your skin, the paper.

I want to write,
Tonight.

That tension
Will kill you
Said no one
Who ever wanted
To help you
"Manage"
Your stress.

A List of Green Flags

This beginning didn't sprout from an ending / I already had my palette cleanser / thank God I didn't waste this plate / my 11:11 wish served on a plater / 11/11 never tasted so sweet / turns out I'm not the black cat following behind the ones who loved me / coffee date, he held the door before he was sure it was me / now he's chasing behind me, grabbing groceries / five dates before I knew I wouldn't fuck it up / asked to kiss you in that studio / it took enough tries for me to get it right / thought I couldn't keep anyone a year, much less four / now I'm ready to tell everyone I'm yours / ready to push my luck a bit farther and ask for you forever.

I've been processing...
I whisper into the phone.
I've been hiding...
I admit to my therapist.
I can't name my emotions
If they are changing faster
Than I can grab a pen,
Spitting nonsense at me
Until I forget my own name,
Much less scrawl prose
Across a constantly shifting page.
I have too many, and too few,
Emotions to tend to.

Outstanding Payments

It is an honor to know Tuesday
Is more of a Monday for you;
To know you'll be home on time
And to talk on all of your breaks.
You've been working so hard
To cover the medical bills in the corner;
You deserve a vacation to Montana
But at least we can drive to Atlanta.

For twenty years before you,
I lived like a cactus, guzzling
Every nicety and giggle, unsure
Of the next trickle or downpour;
The last three years, laughter
Has erupted out of me constantly,
Transformed me into a hot spring.
I apologize if you get burned;
I'm more of a geyser than a spa
But I've been taking more courses
On relaxation, meditation,
Cultivating my garden of Zen;
I've been too nervous to invite you in.

You enjoy sleeping in but between
The cats scratching the kitchen cabinet

And Spring banging on our screen door,
You've been up taking care of us all.
One day, I will buy us a home, just
A bit of land, enough but not too much;
Today, I will put the kettle on for coffee
While you hang dry our laundry.

4/4/2020

Your phone's going off,
Almost as loud as I am;
You're ignoring the messages
To listen to each of my caresses;
I am lying underneath you,
And to several other people.

You learned more about me
Than I knew existed inside me
In the first two weeks
              (Then two years,
                Two thousand lifetimes).

I leant you parts of myself
I never asked to have back,
Buried my anguish in your chest;
You left me with parts of yourself
That no one else at the funeral knew.
I pretended not to know
Your brother's middle name,
Or all the little ways you assumed
You disappointed your mother
(Because what is talking in suburbia?)

You ignored the red flags

I tried to throw in your face,
Held me through waves of blue
Crashing over me on your couch,
Sat with me on that icy night
You saw a familiar grief inside of me,
Tended to it the same way
~~I wish I had done for you~~
I wish you had done for yourself.

I lost you in the snow white nights,
Two hours away;
Every few weeks you'd call
          (Then months,
          It had been years,
          Last year)

Three text messages,
Then five hours before I knew
This was a world without you.
No one ever knew I had you,
The only person I ever told the truth.

It's too cliche to say in a poem
That no one ~~especially not you~~
Will ever read, so let's just say
I wish I could watch those stupid
Fucking cooking shows again.

Good Days (1)

Today I woke up
With an emptiness
In my soul - a hole
That is a whole lot
Easier than a fist
Clutched around it.

Laying my head against
The softness of your shirt,
The warmth of your chest,
The comfort of your heartbeat,
I glance under lashes
At your lips, barely parted.
I want to be a part of them,
Never apart, much less far.

Questions

How was your weekend? / Sunny / What is the weather like? / Fine / How are you coping with late-stage capitalism? / There are poppies popping up in the window sill, herbs still waiting to germinate, and bees eager for the last frost / Are you distracting yourself or are you facing our future in fright? / The mail has only been coming three times a week but our mailman always waves his frail hand when he sees me; I left him calendulas in the newspaper holder / How are you connecting with your comrades? / I've been leaving food in the neighborhood's free fridge / Where do you find community between clock-ins? / Humans are here to indulge in creation, dabble in one another, flirt with the curves and creatures of this terrain / It's magnificent, isn't it?

There was emerald
Everywhere,
Glittering gold globes
Dotted throughout.
Hunkered down
In the honeysuckles
We knew no matter how
Quickly the sun sank,
Darkness couldn't seep
Through all of the green.

I have a nasty routine
Of writing the ending
Before I think of a beginning.
I flip to the last page,
Quick to determine
Our expiration date.

I am tired of spoilers -
Would it unfold any different
If I never knew the ending?
Is my need for control
Constricting us the most?

What if I write in reverse,
Would we walk backward
Until we meet again
At that local coffee shop?
I can still see your smile -

Please, can we stay
In the exposition,
Bypass the explosion?

Stuck somewhere
between
Too Much
and　　　　　far

from enough

My mom was in labor with me
For close to 36 hours -
I was always the most painful
Part of the whole process.
The entire first day
My mom screamed at me
To get the *fuck* out, *now,* please.

The second day, she stared
At the clock, afraid;
April 30th was the birthday
Of her first love, and it wasn't me,
Or my dad.
She clenched her pelvic floor
And gritted her teeth,
Fought with me,
A little pre-me
Who had the audacity
To trigger her trauma.

I entered this world screaming,
Like most of us,
At 12:30 in the morning
On May 1st,
The first of countless
Times I was right on time,
Saving my mom from
Her own temptations,
Even as an infant.

Seeking

There used to be
So many hiding spots.
Now my heart
Is all I've got.

My biggest fear is not
That I am unworthy,
Though it does cross
My mind from time to time.
I am terrified that I am
Unable to give any
Real part of myself away.
My dad used to say
I only knew how
To be vulnerable
In a poem,
And I guess, maybe,
He was right.

Apologies, Apparitions

Six years, six minutes, six months,
They're all jumbled lumps of time,
Meaningless to my grief.
Is there a way to resurrect relationships?
Ways to find the relics of childhood,
Grasp the feeling of being kids one last time,
After all this time?
Is the warmth I feel on my cheeks
When the sun rises through my windows,
Six AM on a Saturday,
Your way of telling me
We are okay?

My fingers crossed
Behind your neck,
Lick my lips
Drip like honey
D
  o
    w
     n
       my thighs.

       Bee's knees,
Oh, please!
Who could believe me
When I am on my knees?

If I Ran a Tea Stand

I would walk around with my mug filled to the brim with two tea
bags of Yerba Mate, a dash of oat milk, and my smile puckering
around the rim / I could mix a smidge of fresh lemon balm in
with a heap of passion fruit, chamomile, and cat nip for the
woman who struggles with insomnia almost as stubborn as mine
/ I would sit in the sun-bathed front window, sipping my second
round of caffeine while waiting for You / You, who stumbled into
my tea shop, unable to articulate what You needed / but bringing
with You Spring / I constantly keep a kettle on, next to pint
packed with lavender, a dash of fennel and a bundle of freshly
dried calendula / in case You ever would / show up here.

What If I Gave You My All?

I dove deep beneath the creek
To get the pollen off my cheeks.

I got caught up in the current
Let the river take my feet;
She dumped me in the ocean
Then left me there to flounder.

In an attempt to ditch the bees
I went swimming with the sharks.

I dove deep beneath the swells
In an attempt to find a shell -
I broke through the billows
With a clam caught in my palm.

THIS IS NOT A POEM, IT'S A LIST OF MY GREED

The Poppy seeds I plant in Spring, no regard for how they'll Fall / the cool brick in our side yard / the combination of peat moss and potting mix where our hands meet / sushi menus with dirty fingerprints / the bits of rice you nibble off my thighs / the rings I try on when you're not looking / the trinket trays carefully arranged for me to play a part / my moms cuffs and pearls plopped in various Goodwill finds / vintage silk Dior dresses for the days my body feels like a vessel for affliction / your undivided attention / to turn into your garden

Sunday Morning

Rising at golden hour to hear
You grinding coffee beans
The clink of a spoon in my mug,
I will leave the dishes
To pile up in the sink,
Sit with you on the back porch,
Survey downtown from a distance,
Before insisting we spend
The whole day doing nothing.

While the question was rhetorical,
I can't hide my amusement
At your reply,
"Every day is Sunday
When you wake up by my side."

I count just over a dozen
Poems written in your honor;
You've set records I never
Meant you to - given me a reason
To search for words again.
Can I memorialize you in every poem
I write from here on out?
You've found a way to define love
In coffee stains rather than purple
Blossoms across my face,
In lots of banging around in the morning
To give me a bit of a warning,
Fighting hard not to fight.
How quickly you filled these pages
With something that resembles light.

I'd go around again,
But only if it's with you.

Does it Make Me Look Needy?

Talk to you on your break / My fingers twirl all day, practicing for their dance up and down your back / The flowers are dropping after a few hours without sunlight / I am the flowers / Even if I bloom, I can't stand tall when without you / My Sun / Drive safe, I can't wait to see you / Come, give me a quick kiss before you unload the day's dishes and gripes / Let my finger pads land on your lumbar / Taste this stew I made for you / Don't be alarmed if I stare I have just missed the image of your sitting there / The rain clouds broke / What my mom called Angel Light shines through just before dusk / Just before / Just one more on my lips / One more one more, please / I love you / Goodnight

I am choosing to love myself,
Selfish as it may be.

Summer

I'm still figuring out
How to create art
Without ripping myself
Completely apart.

Used to it

My past puts her hand
Heavy against my forehead,
Drags me to the dregs,
Swallowed by the tide,
Seaweed wrapping
It's way around my thigh.
How can I kick against
The current when my legs refuse
To listen to my commands?
How can I expect to find
My way back to land
When you stranded me
This far from my humanity?
At this point I am seeking
Air not choked with salt -
I am treading water until I can
Feel my toes tap dance
Against a (fault
        Line) my shoes up
        By the door so I know
        There is always an escape route.

Chronology

I admire the way the light
Hits the dunes, has me confuse
The seasons - are they passing
Rapidly, or am I more absent?
Pull black metal from my against
My abdomen, steady my ever
Shaking hands - if I capture
A moment a day, will they
Feel any less blurry?

I tucked myself neatly into the back row,
Ten minutes late with good intentions;
I was worried you would spot me
If I sat any closer to the stage,
But I couldn't resist seeing a play
Titled *Melancholy*.
I was so wrapped up in emotion,
You were halfway up the aisle
Before I noticed I was the only thing left
Between you and the exit.

I shouldn't have come to the play.

You don't need to say it,
I can feel it, so familiar;
If leaving had been easy,
I would have done it sooner.
I wish I could fold myself up
And fit between the two halves
Of these cheap theatre seats.
I wish that the exit sign
Was three times dimmer;
Then I wouldn't have to see
Your eyes trained on me, simmering.
Sure, this is your university too,
But it was my town long before
You even knew this school existed.

I hate that you stole theatre from me.

I don't get enough credit
For racking up lovers
And leaving them in debt.

I haven't gotten paid
In the praise I deserve
For making men po(o)(u)r

           Their souls out for me.

Stranger's Bedroom

3 AM and I'm
Stumblin'
Tripping into
His bedroom,
Giggling
"I need to feel
The water
Against my skin."
"Are you insane?"
Was he worried
Or annoyed?
Maybe horny?
It's so hard to tell
Why a man is upset.
"Maybe, I think
I can feel my brain
And I need the shower
To wash my thoughts
Right down the drain."
I doubt he'll understand;
We don't speak
The same language,
Even if he's convinced
We do.

Only When I Need to Be

You called me petty
But I'm just tired of men
Who walk all over me.

I got a gym membership
To lie to my parents
When I was spending time
            Working out
With you.

I told my boyfriend
I was at the movies
With my parents,
            And told them the opposite.

To be with you.

Poolside,
Late-night,
Dive right
Into your eyes.

Type

I help men find themselves
When I lose myself in them.
They find girls who look
Just like me, but act
A little less damaged;
Pray tell,
Is their baggage any lighter?

Since I defined their type,
Men date doppelgangers
And pretend it isn't me
They see in their dreams.
No matter the years
I still have you
Wrapped around my pinky;
All I have to do is pull
And you'd be falling through
My phone screen so quickly,
So you'll visit next month?

I forgot how to tread water
When I was in the middle
Of the rising ocean tides;
I gasp at air but only sucked
Bubbles into my lungs
And salt in my wounds.
Wouldn't a little tequila
Be a better coping mechanism
To drown my sorrows in?

She used to tell me
The world was allergic
To me;
Each time I misbehaved
The hives broke out,
The mountains gave out,
Crumbled from my grumbles,
Caused a tsunami to mix
With dish soap in my throat.
No one ever told me
That maybe I was just
Too sensitive
For a world polluted
By the toxicity
Fueling humanity.

Seeking Peace

I used to worry these words
Would one day stop flowing,
But at this point I am fairly certain
They will keep coursing through me
As long as my heart is beating,
Even when I beg them to leave me.

Seven Vices

If I could live off seven vices alone,
I would be a dog with how much I bone;
I'd demand post-coital cigarette breath,
Take ten shots of tequila to-go,
Please don't give me my phone
Lest I dare to descend into drunken
Derision of my demonic, defunct, doxy.
My nails would be nubs, go to type
My card number into my phone
But it only needs my security code.
If I had to pick just one vice
To keep me alive, it would be
The words I write.

Rumors

"What gets passed around,
Must go down,"
They roared.

"The logic is sound,"
He breathed in my ear.

I lost tabs ——————lost track of myself
every time I entered Party Room 414.
Our apartment? Their apartment?
Your apartment.   Spreadsheets,
never you   spread   against me,
all of you against me

I am not delusional - I lived imperfectly.
I hid weed under my mother's urn, forced
myself to burn faster than kindling,
used my heat to attract people to me,
but when I needed a fire escape,
you blocked my way.

                                        When I needed your arms,
I found them wrapped around whoever
was sitting in front of the campfire.

When I needed an extinguisher,
                        I found your roommates slurping
                        Cheerios in front of the cabinet, chuckling.

I found myself in the parking garage,
a puddle on the elevator floor,
four stories below
                Purgatory Quarters 414.

Doppelganger

Am I the sun in her face
When you wake on Sunday?
Or do you reminisce
In the moments her lips
Giggle against your neck?
Was she the first girl you met
Or the first one you found me in?

Is This Survivors Guilt?

I wonder if I hate myself
For the little acts of survival,
Or if the rage is aimed at
The sheer fact I'm still breathing.

The Ones I Would Have Aborted

If my mom's plan to poke holes in my condoms at 15 had succeeded.

If that day I was tired and sick and it-happened-so-quick had done the trick.

If the drug dealer I was fucking at 16 had cum suddenly.

If I realized I was 3 times more likely to have an ectopic pregnancy - which would kill me.

If I had conceived from any of the nearly 100 rapes.

If it broke. If I forgot. If I had an allergy. If I took the pill at an inconsistent time. If my mom poured them into the toilet. If I did everything right. If I did everything wrong. If I used a certain kind of lube. It doesn't matter the issue.

Every single time, if that's what I wanted.

Maternal Infection

You convinced me you were
Allergic to me as a person,
Like my sheer existence
Set off a chain reaction
Inside of you, trying desperately
To flush me from your system
With disregard to my psyche.
Do you know what it's like
For your parent to blame you
For the fact they're dying
To crawl out of their own skin?
To fan the flames just to
Rid themselves of their kin?

I am the one who has been
Abandoned in the detox.

I love when new songs come out,
Because the voices in my head
Finally have something to talk about.

I still haven't figured out
How to tell your story.
I don't want to sugarcoat
The whole thing but
The taste has always been
A bit too bittersweet for me.
Since there is no honest-
To-God truth,
Or at least not one
I am entitled to,
What have I spent
My whole life
Trying to prove?

Bad Night (3)

I broke down
The day I realized
I have to exist
For as long
As this planet
Will have me.

The Color of Closure

I still see the old me,
Flickering in my rearview,
A hologram revealing
How hollow I am,
A shell that used to hold
A soul I couldn't control,
Lit up the night
And burnt boys to a crisp.

I hesitated in the right lane,
Unsure of how to look
Past you rather than at you,
Put the car in reverse,
Forced these shaking hands
To parallel park.

They call you a figment
But could my imagination
Accurately recreate the tides
Contained in your irises?

The only place I see you now
Is frozen in my headlights,
Eyes flashing too fast
For me to catch each bit of blue,

Save it for my rainy days,
Drive through a downpour,
Drive straight out to South Port,
Drive straight off the cliff
So that I can be cradled
By the crashing white caps
Of your eyes, enveloped
In their depths;
Your death drowned me
In sorrows and swells
I was ill-equipped to handle;
I am still wrestling for the wheel.

Places I Have Unexpectedly Found Joy

In clocks constantly moving me further from my trauma / in worm castings coating my hands / in scrubbing clean last year's pots / in wiping down my limbs / in my brain / in the barely-lit corner of my church parking lot, huddled over a pipe in my back seat / at the top of the stairs at the funeral home / in a musty room with an ornate casket / in mom's waxy completion, jagged hairdo she would have despised / in cleansing my hands / in knowing worm food is not capable of abuse.

Compulsion

"I wish you weren't so
Pessimistic,"
They remarked
After complementing
The vulnerability
Expressed in my poetry.
What do you think it takes
To prepare yourself to strip
Down to your core
And transport yourself
To your worst moments
While standing center stage?
Even if I wanted to,
I couldn't have it any other way.

Half of the Time

I say what I mean plainly in poetry / I make quantum leaps in seconds, my brain spinning out towards a black hole before I explode over something seemingly inconsequential / I love with open palms / I love by cutting my own arm off to give you a hand / Give me an emergency God, I haven't stopped dreaming of thinking clearly / Give me a change in plans and I will call on Their wrath / I am filing things alphabetically, by month, by year, by size, by color / I am letting water bottles pile up in my back seat / I have pressed my toes against your ankles, my hand placed on your chest, every inch of me must be connected / I am cooking and boiling over and need three feet plus silence / I am daylight / I am an Alaskan winter.

PMDD

"There has never been
Such a large chunk of debris
Hurling towards the Earth before.
Scientists say they can't be sure
Where the debris from
The Chinese rocket will land."
The news droned on and on;
You thought it was only on
For background noise
When suddenly I exclaimed -
"That's it! That is what I feel like!"
"Like what?" You sounded annoyed,
But then again, everything
Sounds different when you're
Floating through the atmosphere.
"Like I am a heap of garbage,
Discarded and falling
Through zero gravity and
I might smash into anything
Or anyone on my way down!"
I had just gotten started,
No time for slowing down.
"Like... Like I thought I was
Headed into the cosmos
On a mission of my own, only

I was just weighing you down
On your way out of town.
Like I was supposed to think
This through a little farther
And probably a little earlier.
Like I miscalculated my mass,
Made a massive error judgment,
Forgot a self-destruct button
And just hoped for the best,
Or at least an ocean landing.
Like I should be out of breath
Since there's no oxygen in space
And I have been anxiously ranting
Until there's only stardust left in my lungs."
I paused only to gasp for air;
Suddenly your lips were there.

Stretched thin,
The little lines
Across my skin.

Stretched thin,
My last dollars
Across various cards.

Stretched thin,
His never-ending
Patience with my antics.

Red Hot

Red, little light has been
Awake all night,
Heat clutched to my abdomen
And shoved between my thighs.

Red, little light blinking,
Brightly declaring my misuse
Has led to an untimely demise,
Laughing in my face -
No blisters for you today!

Red, blood dripping
Down my lips and legs
As the little dot dances,
Taunting me as I tug
At cords trying to reset
These buttons I have
Over-pressed.

Red, little solid circle
On my stovetop,
A beacon in the pain
To remind me I'm standing,
Still in my kitchen.

Red, hot blotches,
Scars across my stomach,
From hot water bottles
And heating pads
Always pressed against it.

End of Me

It's a good day when
My abdomen is covered
With paper-cuts, peppered
Throughout my insides.

Most days, there are oozing
Blisters, blood boiling
Before pouring into my pelvis,
Feels like acid -

Actually on bad days,
I feel the gashes rip open,
Swell my stomach, pull
At the edge of my wounds

I can feel the inflammation
In the form of daggers dicing
My delicate ligaments, making
Art out of my misery.

Do I need to
Reach a hand
Inside myself,
Scoop out clots
Like ice cream
Melting down
A cone in July?
Do I need to
Let myself faint
Just to see if you
Catch me?
If I pulled out
Photographs
Of the inside
Of my body
And point out
All the chunks
They removed,
Would you begin
To believe in my pain?
Would hitting you over
The head with my cane
Help it to sink in,
Or is it as hopeless
As I think it is?

Self-fulfilling Prophesy

I treat the page
like a confessional,
seek out grief
like it is grace,
put my heart
on display,
center stage,
yet posess
the audacity
to be filled
with such rage.

They laugh,
brush off
"the advocate."

A plotline
older than time.

Chronic

"Writers Block,"
Mocks the spine
Of the journal
On my nightstand.

"Three twenty-seven,"
Taunts the red light
From my alarm clock.

"You always cancel,"
Sneers my insecurities,
Hidden in the last text
My friend sent me.

This Started as an Apology

When we skipped pennies on the lake
Did you expect it to end up this way?
With me skipping through memories,
Forever incomplete?
I am looking for the pieces
To the long forgotten
Puzzle that was my childhood;
Forgive me for crawling beneath
The couch when I know I can't get out -
I was afraid of the raised voices,
One passing moment you didn't witness;
You don't understand the urgency -
I must find the pieces before anyone knows
They went missing - it will be
The death of me.
Oh, you don't know what death
Feels like when it's entering a home?
The creaking of floorboards
And slamming of cupboards,
The clamors and creepy calm?
Then you don't know the sound
Of palms pounding on freckles,
Wood smacking before I have finished bending,
Haven't heard tears hit carpet
And memorized the sound just in case?

My mistake.
I was in the wrong decade.

Have Patience

I don't want to stall,
Wait to write about this
Until it's something of the past,
Fighting for an understanding
Within our ending.

I don't want this to end.

A Dozen Ways to Court a Poet

Be sloppy, making a mess in the kitchen by kissing me in the middle of dinner prep, food left to spoil on the counter in our rush to the bedroom.

Make me laugh, and memorize them all. The boisterous, the
snicker, the snort, the horse.

Be prepared to give all of your forgiveness away

Because I am constantly losing my head, even as it's resting
against your chest; promise me you'll always help me find the
things I'm missing.

Make love to me gently.

Fuck me hard but still

Tell me you think I'm beautiful; I have spent all day wrapped up in the ugliest parts of myself; smudges and grudges accumulate over fifteen years and I fear I will never be done scrubbing my subconscious.

Make time for me to cry (all the time).

I'm tired of begging people to love me, feeling like I have to earn the right to exist when I never asked for any of this.

I'm tired of teaching people how to love me - all it takes is a soft touch of your hand, hushed tones and lighter footsteps. I don't need eggshells but I do require peace.

I'm tired of asking for things. Truth be told, I have no idea what I need.

You love me more than I know how to accept; I just need constant reminders.

Good Days (2)

Today I woke up
With an eagerness
In my soul - a whole
Lot more invigorating
When you wrap
Your arms around me.

Sunday Evenings

I don't want to
Love you in routine;
I want to love you
Recklessly.
Faithfully
Yet sinfully,
I want to dabble
In juxtaposition,
The position
Of your hips,
Lips lingering,
Breath quickening,
Lights dimming.

Unlearning

I am enjoying this   space -
This spite tastes   so sweet,
Your lips   between   my teeth.
I want everything, above
     and beneath;
I want to be the air   you breathe,

     the honey on your tongue,

the bread in your belly,

the feeling in your gut.

I am finally having a once in a lifetime
Love affair with my existence,
Taking myself on dates
(At my therapist's insistence)
Sit by the lake and wait for people
To watch, to write some made-up life,
To laugh at and with;
I am growing more intoxicated
With my own presence every second.

Save yourself,
No one else will

(I have to save
Everyone, or else)

Parking Garage

This poem may be triggering for survivors

Swish swish, clink
Swish swish, clink
Swish swish, clink
Clink clink

Swing the metal door
Back from its hinges,
Struggling against concrete,
Keys scraping against the push bar;
Even the hairs on my arms shudder.

Silence.

The clicking echo
Of a car being locked;
Footsteps mirror my own.

Click, clack, click,
Clack, click, clack,

Cool metal and jagged ridges
Dig their way into knuckle creases;
I watch the cloud of my breath grow bigger

As each inhale I took was quicker.

Click, clack, click,
Clack, click, clack,
A high pitched whistle,

Pause.
Take inventory of my lips,
Still puckered in silence.
Too much silence.

Click clack click
Clack click clack
Click clack click

My steps steadily speed up,
One after another until my hand
Wraps its way around cool aluminum,
Glance through two curtains of curls
Before unlocking the driver's side,
Silently, slipping my way inside,
Whispered prayers held until I jammed
The lock down with my fingers.

Click, clunk.

They say no one
Makes it to adulthood
Unscathed;
At least I survived, right?

Fall

Overcoming

I haven't gone to the dentist
Since I was 16 - 6 years goes by
Quick when you miss 12 visits.
My mom once told me
Dentists are dangerous;
Is it really being gullible
When you're 9 and your mom says
She's just trying to keep you safe?

My mouth has always tasted foul,
My tongue flailing against plaque;
If my connection to the world
Was so disgusting, what does
The rest of me have to offer?

My dentist told me
My wisdom teeth are impacted
But he recommends we leave them -
My teeth are tiny, he said.
No, no that couldn't be right,
What he said was that my teeth
Are incredibly small, he said
He didn't want to hit a nerve
When yanking them out.
No, no he wouldn't haphazardously

Remove bone from my mouth,
If he did complete the surgery
My gums would be carefully resected.
Have I ever met a dentist
Who cracked teeth carefully?

The hygienist had a big mouth -
She scraped and pulled, never tugged
And her voice sounded like a hug
When she told me people pay
Good money to have teeth like mine,
And she never would've guess
Over half a decade had gone by
Had I kept my mouth shut.

Why Do I Blame Myself?

The leaves fell much slower that autumn
Yet you caught me before I caught wind.
I hate you, opening up your heart
Like it's some dive bar, pass me a warm beer.
If we'll be here a while, I might as well
Get comfortable.

You brought brutal honesty,
The silence bounced off ice;
I told God all the time I was thankful,
But truthfully I was just selfish.
You were the warmest body I encountered
Through my worst winter.

The laughter came roaring
Through my grief - like an apparition,
I can still see how it weaved its way
Through grass swaying in the wind
Before it settled, grounded.
Thank God you helped me find the humor.

There was a heatwave that May;
Unfamiliar walls led to the now-familiar
Feeling of your figure pressed against me;
Water breaks and your muscles

Rippled like the waves; I got so lost
In the haze (which is exactly what I wanted).

Somewhere in between plastic cobwebs
And marshmallow rabbits, I missed
The changes in your habits
And you missed the changes in the seasons.
I'm still not sure how to explain it
Even if I know all of the reasons.

all about love
After bell hooks

The central problem is
I didn't know enough
Back then to know
I loved you back when,
When things could
Have been,
Different.
I don't know if you
Understand
Or are even listening;
It has been six years
And I am as forgettable
As you ~~are~~ were forgetful.

I Fall in Love with Ghosts

Swooning as you drove off on your motorcycle / Being the only one to remember your birthday (even now) / Driving the long way across town just to pass by our old hangouts / Meeting your glacial gaze in my rearview / Counting the days since I looked your mom in her vacuous eyes / Reminiscing on days in strangers bedrooms while stuck in your old foyer / Ordering your fast food go-to just to taste a little life again / Tapping the steering wheel to that R&B song you used to always play / Tracing our history with sharpened fingertips, bleeding you into these pages because everyone deserves a chance to fall in love with you.

Kindred Spirit

I'll never forget how you drove
With your foot up by your hip,
Folded up behind the steering wheel.
The sound of your voice, off-pitch,
Still rings in my ears -
I cannot conjure your melodies
This far removed from me,
But I'd know our song anywhere.
The highways and waterways
Fly by with the birds, the views
I know by heart without knowing
Exactly where we are;
The drive to your parents
Hasn't changed since I was born
(Though nothing else remains the same).
There was a carefree spirit
Trapped somewhere inside you;
I hope you found the light
When you left your body behind,
But if you're ever lonely
Know I'm always free for angels.
We can hop inside my hatchback
While we drive (and sing) over
All our favorite bridges.

Mirror Mirror

You pulled yourself
Out of tsunamis
I never witnessed;
You did your best to
Salvage the wreckage
Of a body God
Abandoned you with.

When the waves
Reach my neck
I still reach for you.
As the cool water
Tickles my nostrils,
Your hands wrap
Around my wrist.
These waters can't
Dampen your spirit;
Your spirit has
Never left me.

Untouchable

I will keep writing
Books bound by
Promises I always
Meant to keep;
I will keep writing
About the anger,
But mostly
The forgiveness,
And the regret.
I don't know if
You've had a chance
To read any of them.
I am not sure if
You are as proud
As everyone says
You must be.
I imagine your wings
Chipping as you read
All the demons
You left with me.
I imagine the clouds
Parted to paint you
In a different light,
But you fell
Right through them.

Are my well wishes,
This hand extended
In forgiveness,
Enough to break
Your fall from heaven?
Would God give
You back to me
That easily?
No matter how much
Honesty I crack into
The spine of these books,
There will be
No resurrection;
There will be
The sinking question,
Who is proud of me?
Will the wind
Lick my cheeks,
Drying the tears?
Will it feel more like
Your fingertips
On my freckles
When I finally figure out
How to tell your story?

I wish I could
Have forgiven you
While you were here.
I wish I could
Have held you close
One last time
Without the shards
Of our history
Actively wounding me.
I wish you could have known
I loved you all the same;
Despite all the pain,
I would have loved you again.

Brush Strokes

He slept on the living room couch
In between packing his things
And saying goodbye to me.
The reckoning still makes
Little sense to me,
But it painted a portrait
That colored my love
As I trudged forward -
Endings felt forevermore,
Museums felt full of forgery
Until you were placed
Artfully in front of me.
Perfectly timed,
The afternoon light hitting
Your face just right;
Evening tea turned quickly
To you bringing me coffee
As I curled my legs up
Under your covers.
I found myself captivated by how
The morning light hit your plants,
Shades of green a kaleidoscope
Across your studio and then
I remembered even Picasso
Had a blue period;
We are always becoming
And unbecoming works of art.

I used to think
I was allergic
To people.
Turns out
No one reacts well
To ongoing grief.

I bet she loves
Smashing Pumpkins
And trampling through the Arboretum;
Does she know all those alcoves
You used to pull me into?
Does my scent linger
Just like you do, heavy on her lips?

I bet she loves
Midnight drives and your dive bars,
How your heart is a fragile work
Of tormented art;
Does she know your back roads
And all those lyrical bridges?
Does my voice still find its home
Tucked against your ear drum?

I bet she loves
Her old friends, the same ones
You saw last night, she's missed all year;
Does she know that you've found
Friendship in her best friend's bed?
Do you already know which parts of her
Will cling to you, thick as my perfume?

I bet she loves
Herself, she just forgot how good

It felt, not to always shrink herself;
Does she know that she always
Has a home on my old couch?
Do you know why all of your exes
Now return all of my texts?

"An artist?
In this climate?"

"If not now,
Then when?"

The Gifts at the Top of the Closet

A shoebox with high-top sneakers,
Three packs of chapstick,
A stack of plays I picked up
From the second-hand bookstore
Where we camped out in the stacks,
A gift card to the 24/7 diner
We had to drive an hour and a half
Just to find (which it was just barely
worth the blurry streetlights plus
the 3:20 AM fight on the ride home),
And new guitar picks since I noticed
The dryer ate all your old ones
And your fingers were bleeding
Again. At the top of the load lies
A pile of receipts laughing at me,
Because whoever sticks around
Through my autumns of anguish?

Seasons

I keep thinking I will run out
Of stories to tell from my view,
Stagnant from the couch.
Somehow my psyche keeps
Unearthing new trauma,
Begging me to process it
Right there on the page.
Is this what happens when
You have lived a whole lifetime
Before reaching adulthood?

It's about both
Believing I am
Worth loving
And learning
To give myself
Said love.

In defense of our overgrown garden

We have sorted all of our seeds / I have begun a plant journal, even if I abandoned it half way through the season and only now remembered it existed / We've been tending to our roots, figuring out how to flower with each other's seasons / I have made sure to stay on top of watering this year, pouring into everyone while learning to keep myself full / There might be powdery mildew creeping up on our cucumbers, but our peppers have been blooming all season long / We can always cut back the overgrowth, transform it into compost, let things over winter / In our defense, isn't the whole idea to turn our garden into a forest?

Questions That Feel Like a Hug

Talk on my break?
Do you want coffee or tea?
Have you eaten today?
Want to water the plants with me?
How long have we been doing this?
Which socks match my underwear?
Where do you want dinner?
Want a gluten-free slice?
Can I carry your bag?
Do you want to drive?
Want the first hit?

You and Me

I place a steaming mug
Of honey lavender tea
Next to your wrist,
Poised and ready
For a match to begin;
You glance at me,
More than the computer
Screen lit in your eyes.
Thank you,
Slips from your lips
As easily as agave.

Silk

Silk slides across
Supple lines   and I
Feel like myself
For the first time
In a long time.
Slip into the sheets,
Slide me out of silk,
Come   fill me,
Complete my caverns,
Caress my chest,
And dance your fingers
Up to my neck;
Hold my breath
Between your lips
And tighten your grip.

Addiction

Did you know I tried to quit
At least six times before
You came into my life?
Never lasted much more
Than a month,
Now it's been two years
7 months, 4 days,
9 hours, 47 minutes,
Six, seven, eight seconds...

I Choose You Because

The cats sleep in bed with you, something they'd hesitated to do
with both strangers and long-time lovers alike.

A grin escapes me each morning as I bask in your gaze.

There's excitement in re-thinking intimacy, finally painless for
me, rather than fighting against unwillingness.

Always refilling my water has to be a bother, but you never let it
show.

I like cooking for you, and I like it even more since you appreciate
how good the effort tastes.

I don't have to accompany you to parties to be sure there is
loyalty; in fact, you're more for staying in and I hope that always
remains.

You know how to say the words "I'm sorry," even if you don't
need them very often.

With you, I am always laughing, even if I can't always tell you
why.

I believe you always tell me the truth; I know I could never lie to you (remember that one time I tried to?)

You get goofy instead of grumpy when you're sleepy.

I'm in love with my best friend, and it's finally a reciprocated affection rather than a fatal attraction.

I am finally grasping
The importance
In each of my decisions,
And I am choosing
To give myself to you,
Freely.

Parenting

Curled up on the couch,
Sandwiched between
Two heating pads as
The sweat pools beneath me.
The heat lulls me to sleep,
Only disrupted by the subtle stabs
Of the disease eating away at me.
When my whimpers break
The silence of an empty apartment,
A furry friend finds a home
Nestled against my chest.
I match my breath to his
Gentle purrs and heavy sighs -
There is sanity in feeling
The presence of another,
A witness to your trauma.

I want to fall in love with you over and over again

I wish I could see you from across the street for the very first time (again). I want my smile to burst forth the way it did when I saw you walking towards me that initial winter. I want to pull you in as though I am still desperate to learn the shape of your body. I want to show you that I knew where to tug and pull and kiss and tease before we even met, as though I were created with the ability to please you. I still stare at you on your futon, now in ~~my~~ our living room, see the candle flicker across ridges I have memorized. It still feels like I am falling, like I have never fallen before.

Clear Headed
For Sav

Other addictions were
Far more apparent:
Sticking another cigarette
In between my teeth
Like it is candy;
Pop a few more until
I can feel the Percs
Coursing through my blood;
A couple extra lines
If he lets me take them
Right off his back;
Pass me a dozen white chips,
I have my life to gamble with.
He makes endless promises
Of forever when our breath mixes -
I make the mistake of believing
Every uneven beat of his heart.
This is reckless endangerment,
Forced withdrawal so that when
He comes back I will be desperate
For a little taste (of his lips).
I never understood this knack he had
For keeping me around, until now.

Give yourself
The kind of love
You're desperately,
Depravedly,
Craving.

Meditation

Breathe in,
Breathe out.

Breathe in.
Breathe
        out into the foggy
        afternoon of my mind.
He told me to meet
My life force here
But all I can find is a
        violent black atom,
Spinning ever faster
Towards my very core.

He told me to bring
My life force to the spring,
Let it bathe in the pool,
Let the golden waters
Flood my senses, he insisted -
        Sick and twisted,
        light sucked into darkness
        like it never existed.

I've decided that loving myself
Is the most selfless act of all.

A (Non-Exhaustive) List of Things I Would Miss (Without You)

Talking on the phone every night during your meal break. Someone to always refill my water; someone I'm not afraid to ask for anything. The shape of your smile, a curly bracket. How your lips are constantly, gently upon me. The way the cats run to the door when they hear your car pull into the driveway. Someone who laughs at my dad cracks and putrid puns; someone who lets me in on the joke instead of making one out of me. Learning all of the scientific names for each plant as we pass them in the arboretum. Sticky note lists (on the fridge, under the keyboard, buried in vase above the desk and stuck to every notebook). Falling asleep on the futon on Fridays with the sound of clacking keys and gamer speak fading out behind me. Saturday mornings at the markets (on the rare occasion we are both up and moving by 9). Driving you to the store on Sunday because I can't stand being apart an extra hour and I'd rather spend my morning grabbing more coffee while you gather our groceries. The sound of your breathing deepening, slowly slipping into snores; the comfort of knowing you're there without having to peek through my eyelashes. The sound of coffee being ground for me in the morning.

Good Days (3)

Today I woke up
With a contentment
In my soul - a whole
Lot more complete
Now that I believe
I am worth loving.

Acknowledgements

Queer Views: From the Other Side: Finding Out

Word: Volume XIII: Inventory

Queer Views: From the Other Side: Guardian

Fox Paw Literary Blog: Cavities

COALESCE Community: Outstanding Payments

Olit Magazine: Questions

Other Worldly Women Press: My mom was in labor with me

Resurrection Magazine: What if I Gave You My All?

Meow Meow Pow Pow Lit: THIS IS NOT A POEM, IT'S A LIST OF MY GREED

The Vital Spark: PMDD

Sunday Mornings at the River: Red Hot

Wishbone Words: End of Me

Wishbone Words: Chronic

The Abbey Review: This Started as an Apology

The Elevation Review: Brush Strokes

trouble maker fire starter: Silk

Maggie Bowyer (they/them/theirs) is a poet, cat parent, and the author of various poetry collections including *Ungodly* (2022) and *When I Bleed* (2021). They are an essayist with a focus on Endometriosis, chronic pain, and trauma. They have been featured in Bourgeon Magazine, Capsule Stories, Plainsongs Poetry Magazine, The Abbey Review, Troublemaker Firestarter, Wishbone Words, and more. They were the Editor-in-Chief of The Lariat Newspaper, a quarter-finalist in Brave New Voices 2016, and they were a Marilyn Miller Poet Laureate. You can find their work on Instagram and TikTok @maggie.writes.

CPSIA information can be obtained
at www.ICGtesting.com
Printed in the USA
BVHW052341190123
656708BV00018B/150